# WHAT YOUR TEACHERS DIDN'T TEACH YOU

## How to Get a Job After College

### (A Manual)

## GAILYA SILHAN

ISBN: 1-4392-6509-7
ISBN-13: 9781439265093

For my two best graduates, Troy and Caitlyn

. . .

# TABLE OF CONTENTS

Gailya Silhan

"The first duty of a human being is to assume the right functional relationship to society – more briefly, to find your real job and do it."

Charlotte Perkins Gilman

. • •

Gailya Silhan

# TEN REASONS YOU WON'T GET HIRED WHEN YOU GRADUATE:

- You waited too long to start your search.

- You didn't do your homework. As a recent graduate, you were virtually born with a computer in your hands, yet you didn't research the company.

- You don't know how to network—not enough people know you're looking for a job.

- You posted your resume online, and are waiting for the phone to ring.

- Your resume sucks—three pages of jobs that don't relate to your field, your 3.2 GPA, and improper personal details.

- You have no business etiquette. Your manners are poor, you dress too casually, your online identity is, excuse the pun, sophomoric.

- You blow the interview—talk too much, don't have relevant questions, ask about money/vacation at the first meeting.

- You have no follow through.

- Your requirements are too high for an entry-level employee.

- You don't know how to "close"—ask for the job.

BUT I GET AHEAD OF MYSELF...

Gailya Silhan

# FROM THE AUTHOR

First of all, let me say that I have worked closely with Career Centers and Advisors at the college level, specifically those at SMU (as a mentor and speaker), and at Boston University (as a parent of a student). They work tirelessly to assist each and every student refine their choice of major, their resumes, their presentation skills and more. My impetus for writing this book was the realization that most universities have tens to hundreds of thousands of students and not all of them will avail themselves of the college resources.

I am thirty years into a career that I virtually "fell into." I grew up in the south. I graduated from high school and applied to three colleges, and was accepted by two. Then my boyfriend asked me to marry him and college was put on hold. Fast forward four years and I was divorced, working as an administrative assistant, and not making enough to support myself. I interviewed and was hired as an Account Executive at a radio station.

I became a manager seven years into my career, overseeing eight AEs and having the responsibility of meeting and exceeding budget for a radio station in a top ten market. This was my first experience hiring as well. I wasn't very good at it!

Since that first management job, I have interviewed, hired, and fired many, many employees, including some recent college graduates. Along the way, I had the benefit of some great mentors and employers who shared their experience with me. In writing this book, I have included some of their favorite stories of both the best and worst interviews. I've also had the very good fortune to know and work with some of the leaders in the fields you may be considering—business, finance, web design and management, advertising agency creative and brand management, and the music business. They, too, have shared their experiences.

Times have certainly changed since my good fortune brought me to my dream career. You have the benefit of a college education. I'm sure you're bright and motivated, but you lack experience. You've been told that you have the unfortunate luck of graduating from college at just the time when we've gone from losing six hundred thousand jobs a month to a "mere" two hundred fifty thousand. Jobs are scarce.

**That may be true, but people ARE getting hired. We just have to make sure it's *you*.**

. . .

# WHAT TO EXPECT
# FROM THIS BOOK...

*"I know the price of success: dedication, hard work, and an unremitting devotion to the things you want to see happen."*

Frank Lloyd Wright

• • •

Gailya Silhan

Will this book help you get a job in the next two weeks? I hope so. But chances are that it will take you ninety days to six months to find a suitable position.

I know you want shortcuts; you want a fail-safe way to get to the end game. The truth is, finding a job IS your job right now. Dedicate a number of hours daily to the task (four or five should be good)—to researching, making phone calls, writing notes, interviewing. Then meet with friends who are in the same search mode to exchange stories and support each other.

Keep paper with you at all times – write down anything that strikes you while you're in this search. You may see an advertisement, read an article, talk to a stranger, or just have a random thought that needs to be saved. Do not confine your efforts to the time you're writing resumes or making calls. When Albert Einstein was working on a problem that seemed unsolveable (like the theory of relativity), he would leave his office and take a long walk. When he returned, he often had the equation in his head and could make it work!

This is your first test of post-college life.

Gailya Silhan

# KNOW THYSELF!

*"Knowing others is intelligence; knowing yourself is true wisdom. Mastering others is strength; mastering yourself is true power."*

*Tao Te Ching*

. . .

Gailya Silhan

I'm going to ask that you not skip ahead as you read.

There are times when I will give you an exercise—and your willingness to complete these will pay off in the long run.

I know you're tempted to go to the chapter you want to read most, but I assure you that you will get more out of it if you proceed one step at a time.

## EXERCISE ONE:

Find a quiet place to think. This shouldn't take more than ten to fifteen minutes.

On the left side of the page, list all of the things you've been proudest of, since your earliest memories.

For example, my first was being transferred to a grade school in our new hometown only to find that all of the students had been through kindergarten, which I hadn't. The class was divided into "A," "B," and "C" reading and math groups and I was placed in the "C" group. I was crushed! I worked every night for some time to get into that "A" group. It was my life's work at the tender age of six, and I succeeded.

Your proud moments may be similar, or they may be around sports, being a young entrepreneur, your contributions to a team, earning your Eagle Scout award, and so on. Please complete *Proudest Moments* before you continue.

# EXERCISE ONE:

## **Proudest Moments:**

1. _____

2. _____

3. _____

4. _____

5. _____

BONUS QUESTION:  Describe a difficulty or challenge of some magnitude that you've experienced – then describe how you overcame the challenge (think specifics).

Now, fill out "What It Means".  My page would look like this:

| Proudest Moments | What It Means |
| --- | --- |
| 1. Made it to "A" group | Determination, perseverance, competitive, hard worker |
| 2. Honors math in middle school | Competitive, desire to succeed |
| 3. Got my first job w/o parent's knowledge as a teacher's aide | Industrious, wanted to work, loved opportunity to earn my own money |
| 4. Graduated high school with honors (my dad promised me a car!) | Goal-oriented, long-term plan, monitored each semester |
| 5. Landed job in radio sales with no experience and advanced to #1 within a year | Willing to take a risk (this was a commissioned job) a fast starter, highly motivated to succeed and earn money, competitive |
| 6. Youngest General Manager in Dallas radio history | Recognized as highly capable in my field, driven, able to manage. |

**Now, translate your proud moments into what they mean:**

1. _____

2. _____

3. _____

4. _____

5. _____

## HOW TO TRANSLATE THIS INFORMATION TO YOUR PROSPECTIVE EMPLOYERS

Now you've identified some tangible traits that mean something to you. Whether your proudest moments revolved around sports achievements, church, community service, or academics, you have likely found that there are similar themes that have strung these experiences together.

First, you need to OWN this information about yourself. It's in your DNA; you just haven't put a name to it before now!

Next, think about ways to incorporate some of this information into your one-minute pitch, cover letter, and interview (more on these to follow). You may even put it on your resume (though not under work experience) if you feel you can pull it off.

Go with confidence!

Gailya Silhan

# RESEARCH

*"Whenever you are asked if you can do a job, tell 'em,
"Certainly I can!" Then get busy and find out how to do it."*

*Theodore Roosevelt*

• • •

Gailya Silhan

Because you have no pre-computer memories and spend a great deal of time online, it's natural to post a generic resume on job sites such as www.Monster.com, www.Yahoo!Jobs.com, or www.CareerBuilder.com. In my experience, these sites are **highly** unlikely to yield results. You need to put a little more work into it.

I cannot over emphasize this next step—prospective employers hate interviewing a candidate who doesn't know about their business!

## EXERCISE TWO: Some Basics

Make a list of companies where you would like to work. You may get leads from parents, friends of parents, professors, advertisements, while reading the newspaper(s) and trade magazines, or simply by reputation.

Go to each company's website and look at their product line, their "leadership," their annual report (if published here), number of employees, cities/states they have offices, their press releases, and job openings. Note: Most sites have short bios on their executives—find one in the area of your expertise and read it. You may reach out to this person later. Either print the pages or write the info down!

Go to an information site such as www.hoovers.com, www.vault.com, www.wetfeet.com, or www.ceoexpress.com. None of these will substitute for the company's own website, but they give you basics including the phone numbers at headquarters. On some, you should be able to click on "Competitors," which gives you more places to research and consider, as well as information to have on hand if you interview with the company (employers like to know you're familiar with their business, including their primary competition). If you are in

Finance, go to www.forbes.com.  If you are in Marketing, go to www.adage.com.  Get it?

I found the following information on the Verizon Wireless website:

Summary: Like most leading-edge technology companies, Verizon is eager to hire recent graduates from every field. The starting salaries are limited, but Verizon subsidizes major opportunities for training and advancement.

Fields Hiring: Any and all.  They are actively recruiting trained Java programmers and bilingual (English/Spanish) technical and sales personnel.

Average Compensation:  Salaries of $25,000 and above is the reliable starting point for a college graduate with no experience.

Training: They offer extensive job training and provide, free of charge, classes in Business Writing, Career Planning, Project Management, Technical Data Management, Sales, and Marketing. For details, see http://www.vzwcareers.com/Why/Train.aspx.

Store Locations: Texas, including Houston, Dallas, and San Antonio, Oklahoma, including Oklahoma City and Tulsa

• • •

**TRUE STORY**

Horace Blake, Senior Field Human Resources for FedEx Ground, had this to say, "Frequently applicants show up for open calls on a specific job, then during the interview ask 'What position am I interviewing for?' They nonchalantly do this in hopes they could get a job that is not even available."

• • •

Gailya Silhan

# YOUR SKILL SET, OR WHAT YOU ALREADY KNOW HOW TO DO

*"Nothing in the world can take the place of persistence. Talent will not; nothing is more common than unsuccessful men with talent. Genius will not; unrewarded genius is almost a proverb. Education will not; the world is full of educated derelicts. Persistence and determination alone are omnipotent. The slogan, 'press on' has solved, and always will solve, the problems of the human race."*

*Calvin Coolidge*

• • •

# EXERCISE THREE:  CIRCLE ALL THAT APPLY

**Accounting**
Budget Planning
Capitalization
Cost Accounting
Cost/Benefit Analysis
Finance Management
Special Projects
General Ledger
Internal Controls
Payroll
Reporting

**Administration**
Communications
Customer Service
Event Planning
Multi-tasking
Project Management

**Advertising**
Branding
Copy Writing
Direct Mail
E-Commerce
Internet Marketing
Media Buying
Media Planning
Media Relations
Public Relations
Merchandising
Presentations

**Finance - Commercial Banking**
Credit Analysis
Marketing/Sales Skills
Product Design & Market
    Segmentation
Financial Engineering
Foreign Exchange Derivatives
Very Strong People Skills
Broad Knowledge of Accounting

**Finance - Corporate**
Analytics
Problem Solving
Accounting
VBA Macro in Excel
Reuters or Bloomberg
    Station

**Presentation Skills**
Word
Power Point
Excel
Public Speaking
Special Formatting
Photoshop

## Sales & Marketing
New Business Development
Account Mgmt
Client Relations
Cold Calling
Generating Leads
Needs  Analysis
Presentations
Product Launch
Sales Promotions

## Technology
Business Analysis
Help Desk
Technical Writing
Infrastructure Design
Internet/Intranet
Standards & Concepts
IT Security
Network Design
Network Administration
Process Development
Research
Software Development
System Analysis
System Design
System Installation/Integration
Web Design

## Supply Chain Management
Distribution
Inventory Control
Logistics
Outsourcing
Procurement
Quality Control
Shipping / Receiving
Vendor Relations
Manage / Prevent Shrinkage

## Telecom Engineering
Configuration Experience
NCTA Familiar
Support for IPT Systems
Customer Service
Network Installation
Knowledge of Telephony
USTA Familiar
ITU Familiar
IETF Familiar
NECA Familiar
Operate Network Equipment
Doc/Change Process
Management

You should use the skills you've circled in your resume. Often candidates don't include the fact that they are proficient at Excel or Photoshop, but employers want to know. This exercise may have pointed out that you need to gain some skills as well. It is by no means all-inclusive, but an exercise to get your mind and process going in the right direction.

# BUILDING YOUR RESUME

*"All great masters are chiefly distinguished by the power of adding a second, a third, and perhaps a fourth step in a continuous line. Many a man has taken the first step. With every additional step you enhance immensely the value of your first."*

*Ralph Waldo Emerson*

• • •

Writing a resume has been the subject of many books, websites, and classes. It's not brain surgery, but some of the finer points may help yours float to the top of the stack versus the bottom.

## Heading

This is simplicity itself—centered name, address, phone, and email address. Make sure your email is not sigmagirl@hotmail.com or surferdude@gmail.com. Now is the time to have a business email—josephsmith@gmail.com.

## Objective

Broad statements such as "Work in a company where I can utilize my skills/degree," or "Work in a challenging environment, increasing the sales/productivity of the company" won't cut it. And phrases that used to be cutting edge are now used too frequently, including "results-oriented" and "proven track record."

Yours, coming right out of college, should be a direct statement relating specifically to the job position you seek. For example, "I am seeking a position as a Telecommunications Engineer," or "I am seeking a position as a Project Manager." If responding to an ad, use the exact wording as the position you are seeking.

## EXERCISE FOUR:

I am seeking a position as_____ (be specific).

You fill in the blank. This is actually a good exercise, as it requires that you KNOW what position you seek. One of employers' biggest gripes is that candidates don't know what they want to do, what job they are actually seeking and why. If YOU don't know, how are they to find a fit for you in their organization? If you are sincerely at a loss for the answer, set up some informational interviews with several different companies to discuss jobs within your field. It will give you information as well as clarity.

## Chronological Work Experience

This is a challenge for new college graduates. If you've interned in your field, you have relevant work experience. If you haven't, you need to list your accomplishments/jobs in an effort to demonstrate what you can bring to the company.

*Example:* A student with a degree in business, who has not interned with a relevant company, can still create a decent work history.

Sept 2008 – Present  Laundry Service, SMU
After ascertaining a clear need for it, I created a laundry service for students at SMU. I negotiated rates with an industrial laundry service and created an on-campus business. The business was generating $5,000 per month in profit when I graduated.

Sept 2007 – Dec 2009  Algebra II Teaching Asst
As a requirement of my scholarship, I tutored students in this class in an effort to help them pass the course. I also graded papers for my professor.

June 2005 – August 2008  McDonald's  Part-Time Manager
Started as cleaning crew and was quickly promoted to cash register. I worked there for four summers, ultimately as a part-time manager who opened and closed the restaurant when necessary, and was responsible for receipts as well as scheduling employees.

Note: If this student HAD interned, this would be the place to list those experiences. Stress responsibilities and skills that are relevant to the prospective employer you are preparing to meet.

## Education
Bachelor of Science, Business, SMU, 2010. (No GPA unless it's 3.5 or better. Personally, I prefer no GPA be listed unless you're in the top 10 percent of the class.)

*Study Abroad:* <u>Be very careful here</u>! Unless you can illustrate what you did specifically and/or *what skills you acquired that you can translate into benefits to your employer*, it is better to steer clear of this one.

*Acceptable*: Summer Semester 2009, Niger, Africa
I worked with local NGOs to understand how international foundations operate. I worked with local attorneys to broaden my understanding of a legal system outside the United States (this student majored in Political Science and went on to law school).

*Sorority/Fraternity:* Do NOT put this information on your resume unless you held a position which required leadership skills (Did you successfully raise money for events? Were you an officer and, if so, what were your duties? Etcetera, etcetera). If you are certain the prospective employer is (a) an alumni of your school or (b) was a member of your organization, you may include the information. Many executives do not share the Greek system experience and will not value it.

## Other Interests
This is the place to list association memberships (if you aren't a member of an organization in your area of expertise, join one!). Also, volunteer activities are viewed positively.

## Professional References
Often, interviewees put "Available Upon Request," but at this stage of your job search, it's good to furnish them upfront.

It will show that you came prepared. It is best to use the managers you reported to as an intern, but lacking that, you can use the managers at summer jobs.

Make sure to clear it with anyone you list. You need to furnish their name, position, company, and telephone number and/or email address.

## Personal References
Resist the urge to use family members in this section. Professors, someone from a group you have participated in such as church, on-campus organizations, and so on are acceptable. Provide the same information as you would for professional references.

## Notes
Your resume should be a *single page*, printed on white or cream linen stock. You can easily have these printed at Staples, Office Depot, or Office Max. Do a different resume for each job description you apply for, paying close attention to what you may need to add or delete based on the company, the person who will be conducting the interview, and the research you've already done.

Do NOT include a picture of yourself unless you hope to become a realtor, where it is considered acceptable. Seriously, it immediately dumbs down the resume, especially if you are a young woman!

Gailya Silhan

# BEFORE THE INTERVIEW - HAVING A PLAN

*"I'm a great believer in luck and I find the harder I work, the more I have of it."*

*Thomas Jefferson*

• • •

## EXERCISE FIVE:

**You must clean up your online identity.** Google your name and see what comes up. Anything that doesn't feature you as an ideal candidate for a job in the industry you are seeking needs to be deleted. That includes facebook.com, myspace.com, youtube.com, and so on—no pictures of parties, no political views, no vulgarity.

Next, you need to create a professional online identity. Linkedin.com is the foremost site for businesspeople. Create a profile and join a professional group in your field. Create a ZoomInfo.com account as well. Most corporate recruiters and approximately 20 percent of headhunters in America have ZoomInfo accounts. Recruiters/headhunters go to ZoomInfo and type in the requirements they need—skill set, degree, city, functional title, etcetera. Then they may go to LinkedIn and run the same search.

After you've cleaned up your online identity, you can use the web to your advantage. For example, you can go to GoDaddy.com and create your own URL, using your name as the domain. If you have a name that is fairly common (find out by Googling yourself), find a way to separate it from the pack. Use first initial, last name or first initial, middle name, last name or use a hyphenated last name that includes your mother's maiden name and your last name. Post your resume here and recruiters may have the opportunity to find you in their searches. On any email signature, include the link to your website as well as your LinkedIn profile.

Computer searches are done by keywords. Find several that apply to a search someone might be doing on a position you would like. For example, if you want to work for a "big four" accounting firm, some of your keywords might be financial, analyst, accounting, etcetera.

Sign up for a free Google Profile. It gives you some control on what people see when you appear on Google. Find blogs that are trusted and contribute, create your own blog, and when you post on a blog, make sure to invite your social network to view. You may even forward it to other bloggers who have large followings. The goal is to be in as many (appropriate) places as you can.

Ideally, you should begin your job search during the last semester of college (or earlier). The throngs of graduates in January and June create a much larger field of competition, so your strategy should be to start networking, setting up informational interviews, and set yourself up for a job as soon as you graduate.

## Your One-Minute/Three-Minute Pitch

You will need to prepare what you're going to say when you are calling for an interview or networking. Think of this as a mini-verbal resume. Write it out and get comfortable with it. Some people like to memorize it—I personally like to have four to six bullet points in my notebook that I can verbalize. Here's an example:

> "I am a recent graduate of SMU Cox School of Business. I've been working since I was nine, selling lemonade, cleaning yards, and as I got older, managing projects for a builder. I've interned for XYZ, ABC, and 123, and understand the business from several perspectives. The common thread of all my education and experience is this: I love to work. I love to learn. I welcome challenges. *And I like to win!*"

## EXERCISE SIX: Writing Your Three-Minute Pitch

_____

_____

_____

_____

_____

_____

**Networking**

Networking is a little like public speaking—I meet a lot of people who are afraid to network. Basically it's like working a phone tree. You don't know the person at the top or bottom, but there are a dozen people on the tree who do. Your goal is to fill in the blanks.

The process is meeting new people and sharing a one-minute or three-minute pitch in the hopes that they will share their contacts. When networking, you must be willing to share, so ask yourself what value you have to someone. For example, you know someone hiring in your new contact's field, so you give him the heads up or you recall a news story about the business and use it as a place to start a conversation. Even if you don't have common ground, don't be afraid to tell him that you are looking for a position as _____ (fill in specific title) and, after getting to know him, ask if he knows anyone hiring. Generally, people enjoy being helpful.

You must also listen...*actively*! The person you've just met has a story to tell, and would be more willing to help you if you genuinely wanted to learn about him or her. Next, exchange business cards. I can hear you saying, "What business card, I don't have a JOB!" Get a basic business card featuring your name, phone number, and email address. You may also want to add "BS, Business SMU 2009" and "Seeking a position as Project Manager" (you adapt to your degree and the position you are seeking). Have these printed at Kinko's, Staples, or Office Depot on white or cream stock.

> **Joseph Smith**
> BS, Business  SMU 2009
> Seeking Position as Project Mgr
> 214.555.1212
>
> jsmith@gmail.com

(Don't get artistic with your cards. They are to convey basic information.) Now make a note on the back of each card you receive and make sure to put it in a pocket separate from where you keep YOUR cards. You don't want to hand your friend's card to someone you are introducing yourself to! After any networking event, take the time to email the contacts you've made.

By the way, ALWAYS have your cards with you—and give them to anyone and everyone you can who might help in your search for a job.

## More Networking Basics

Make a list of people who know you're looking for a job. Then make a list of people who SHOULD know. That second list is important. It should match up with decision-makers at companies you're targeting. Take steps to make sure they know who you are—internal referrals, local career fairs, alumni contacts, even cold calling (see "Finding the Decision Maker").

Go to trade luncheons, meetings, and conventions! Even before you join, you can usually get a ticket or invitation to one of these functions. Take business cards, mingle, and introduce yourself. Do NOT try to get an appointment for a job interview in this setting. This is the "set up for the shot." Also, have some information on what's happened recently in your industry, or in the speaker's company, or from the trades, so you will have something pertinent to add to the conversation.

If you develop a relationship with ANYONE in your industry, ask him or her if they know anyone who is hiring. If they say yes, get the name and number, and (heads up, this is important) ask if you can use your contact's name as an introduction. Repeat. Repeat. Repeat. **This may be the single most productive**

**step you can take in your job search. Referrals are priceless.**

• • •

*My Own True Story:*
When I moved from Dallas to Los Angeles, I was a General Sales Manager at a top ten radio station in the number five market in the U.S., with over nine years experience in my field. I moved to accommodate my husband's transfer, and my company did not have a station in L.A., so I started looking for work. The managers in L.A. weren't interested in my background; they said they needed someone with relationships with their customers. It took me three months of solid networking to get my foot in the door in that market. Like most fields, it was a tight-knit community.

• • •

Gailya Silhan

# FINDING THE DECISION MAKER

*"Don't waste life in doubts and fears; spend yourself on the work before you, well assured that the right performance of this hour's duties will be the best preparation for the hours and ages that will follow it."*

*Ralph Waldo Emerson*

• • •

Finding the decision maker may be the single most difficult pre-interview step in finding a job. Websites and trade magazines often list the CEO, CFO, and COO, but it's not likely you will be interviewing at that level. You will find that administrative assistants are either your best friends and allies or total roadblocks to the person with which you wish to speak.

## Tactic One – Establish Contact and Get E-Mail Address

Cold call the company and, without identifying the purpose of your call, ask who the _____ manager is and how to spell his or her name. Ask if they have an assistant, then ask for that person's name and if you could be transferred to them.

When you reach the assistant, introduce yourself and ask if you could have the manager's email address. If they ask for more information before they're able to give it to you, tell them you're about to graduate from SMU and you are putting together information on the industry. You hope to get the manager's assistance. (This is true—your first interviews are likely to be informational.) If you simply obtained the email address of the manager, send him or her an email with the same request. Most executives will share their experience with young people—and most everyone likes to tell their story and talk about themselves!

Note: Treat every assistant as if he or she IS the employer. Be friendly. I once hired a young man with no experience in my field because of his friendly persistence. My assistant loved him and was his advocate—and I always sought her input. How someone treats your assistant tells you a lot about them.

• • •

> *True Story:*
>
> Evan Harrison is a Senior Vice-President with Clear Channel who is responsible for the website content of over one thousand radio properties across the country. Evan started in the record business, was hired by AOL to help them establish a music presence, and then he moved to Clear Channel.
>
> His advice: "Be relentless and persistent. It's a fine line between being aggressive and being a stalker…straddle it with class. Show respect to certain formalities—dress up for the interview, use proper grammar in emails, etc. Offer to work for free. Prove yourself, ask how you can 'get in,' and articulate WHY you want to get in." What does he detest? In a word, "Entitlement."

· · ·

## <u>Tactic Two – Spring For a Cuppa Coffee</u>

Okay, you can't get through to the assistant or the manager. Call and ask for someone in the department you hope to join. Tell them who you are and that you'd like to buy them a cup of coffee and learn a little about the field/business. When you meet, make sure you ask about the company culture—often people at your level will be very forthright about the best and worst company traits. Ask how you can get in to see the manager for an interview. Make a friend!

• • •

## Tactic Three – Six Degrees of Separation

It's true; there are few connections in business or nature that are separated by more than six degrees.  In this instance, it will be people who know the manager you're hoping to meet.  Ask your parents, their friends and associates, your professors, and so on, if they know the person you're trying to see and if you can use their name by way of introduction.  Then your email subject line can read, "per John Jacobs."  It will get you past the automatic delete button of unfamiliar emails.  Wait one to two days before following up with a phone call, but no longer.

• • •

## Tactic Four – FedEx

When totally shut out, I send information via FedEx. It's more likely to be put on the person's desk than regular correspondence. Where the FedEx form asks you to put "From," put your first initial and last name, nothing more.

At best, he or she reads it and remembers your name. At worst, you can now call his/her office and say honestly that you are following up on a FedEx sent on (date).

Wait a maximum of two days before the follow up phone call.

• • •

## Tactic Five – The In-Person Approach

Call the office and ask for the manager's assistant's name. Go to the office with your resume in a sealed envelope for him/her. Hopefully he/she will come to the lobby to accept the "package." You can hand it off personally along with your business card. Try to engage them in a two to three minute conversation.

"Can you please get this to Mr. Davis?"
"Is there a good time for me to call Mr. Davis to follow up?"
_____ (your turn)

• • •

> **True Story:**
> Brenda Adriance, former GM of KISS 106.1 in Dallas, had this to say, "Handwritten notes will help you stand out. A note is great, but gifts aren't. I once received a bouquet of flowers from an interviewee. It made me think he wanted a date, not a job."
>
> Note: No gimmicks. There was a time, long, long ago, when people did "cutesy" things like send one shoe to the manager with a note: "Just trying to get my foot in the door," or send a crisp dollar bill (or larger) with a note "I can help you increase your bottom line," and so forth. That was then. This is now. **Don't do it**.

# KNOW YOUR INTERVIEWER

*"The great successful men of the world have used their imagination…they think ahead and create their mental picture in all its details, filling in here, adding a little there, altering this a bit and that a bit, but steadily building – steadily building."*

*Robert Collier*

You cannot be 100 percent accurate in assessing the communication style of your potential employer, but with the following information, you can tailor YOUR communication to them in such a way that they accept it most easily.

For example, if you reach someone (assistant, boss, whoever) who is abrupt and very straight forward, you are likely dealing with the **Doer**. You need to be ready to get to your point quickly. State who you are and what you are hoping to accomplish: "Yes, Mr. Davis, I'm Joseph Smith and I'd like to see if we can set a time for me to meet with you regarding an Assistant Marketing Manager position in your firm." If he says he doesn't have time, ask if you can email him (I often email high-level decision makers *before* I call them. It allows them the freedom to respond when they have the time—and it allows me to reference the email when I am trying to get past a particularly skilled gate keeper.) If he sounds annoyed or distracted, ask if there is a more convenient time for you to call. If you do score an appointment, be very prepared with resume in hand, answers for likely questions, and questions for him.

If you reach someone who is friendly right off the bat, you are probably talking to the **Communicator** or the **Agreeable**. The **Communicator** will be naturally upbeat and have a positive energy that is hard to miss. An **Agreeable** is friendly, but more subdued. Either way, advance with courtesy and you will likely get the opportunity to meet or email him or her. You can even make a humorous remark to engage them. If you do score the appointment, be just as prepared for these two as you were for the **Doer**. As you talk more, the **Communicator** will share anecdotes, smile or laugh, and engage you in conversation. (Caution – their friendly approach may disarm you into sharing more than you should.) An **Agreeable** will likely let you do most of the talking unless you engage him or her with questions. Do it!

If you reach someone who sounds a little distant, and/or asks for information up front, you may have met the **Thinker**. These folks thrive on data and information. Be sure to provide it, both via your resume and by things you have researched about the company. This decision maker will want to know that you have all the facts at hand. They may seem unfriendly— they are often not very social.

Gailya Silhan

# DEFINING THE INTERVIEWER'S STYLE:

### The Doer

Direct and to the point

Not social until they know you

Works from both information and gut

Weighs pros and cons

Makes decisions quickly

Needs to be respected and recognized as a leader

### The Thinker

Thrives on information

Needs support (data, referrals, research)

Agonizes over decisions

Needs to feel safe

### Communicator

Wants to get to know you

May have family pics displayed

Exchanges information freely

Somewhat impulsive

Likes teamwork

Smiles and laughs often

### Agreeable

Wants to be liked

Will say they have to think about it

Makes it hard to find and answer objections

Won't make decision alone

If you haven't noticed already, note that the two decision-maker types on the left side of the page make decisions fairly quickly.  The ones on the right are very process-oriented and you will have to talk with and see them repeatedly before they arrive at a decision.

The two decision-maker types on the top of the page need information (the Thinker more than the Doer).  They are skeptical of people who shower them with compliments and they do not need others' approval.  The two on the bottom are more feeling-oriented.  No one is in one quadrant alone, but they do have a dominant style.

• • •

***True Story:***
    J. Carrell, Wealth Management Advisor at Smith Barney, shared his own experience with me.  Jay told me that most advisors at Smith Barney are not hired directly out of college, but come in from other firms.  He said, "I contacted the branch manager directly and went through six months of interviews with him and several other individuals before I received an offer."

Think he might be in a field where most decision makers are **Thinkers**???

• • •

# FINALLY, THE INTERVIEW!

*"Calmness is the cradle of power."*

*John Gilbert Holland*

• • •

Gailya Silhan

# TOP TEN WAYS TO BLOW THE INTERVIEW

#10. You don't ask for feedback from the interviewer.

#9. You don't "close" before you leave the appointment.

#8. Your mannerisms are annoying.

#7. You don't have intelligent questions to ask the interviewer.

#6. You answer the interviewer's questions, but without focusing the answer on what the interviewer has told you he needs.

#5. Your resume is not tailored to the position, is too long, or has misspelled words or incorrect grammar.

#4. You dressed wrong for the company culture.

#3. You're unprepared.

#2. You're desperate (they can always tell!)

#1. You're LATE.

## Prep, Prep, Prep!

By this point, you've already researched the company, gone to their website, read their press releases, and learned about their competitors. They have your resume and have called you in for an interview—eureka! Success! Not so fast…

Plan this like a great dinner party. Know whom you will be meeting and if there will be more than one person. Learn the correct pronunciation of their names. Dress for it, get excited about it, and put yourself out there!

· · ·

**True Story:**

Diane Fannon of The Richards Group told me about one of the worst interviews in her experience…, "I set an interview with a young lady who was set to graduate in a few weeks. She was referred to me by a former colleague. Twenty minutes into the interview, I knew she hadn't been looking for a job—but she believed she'd have one by the end of August. She didn't write anything down, even when I gave her the name and number of our HR person and told her it would be a good idea to contact her."

· · ·

Dress according to the company's personality. Safer to go slightly more conservative versus more relaxed. In finance, banking, law, and other traditional fields, a suit and tie for men and a jacket over a skirt or pants for women is appropriate. You can show your personality by your selection of your tie or accessories. On women, in particular, unique accessories lead to being remembered. Just remember scale and don't wear "bling."

Think of someone you admire in the business world and emulate him or her—look at what they wear, how they present themselves and how they act/speak, then tailor some of it to suit you. Your "costume" will give you confidence.

Don't be offended when you read this…it may well be time for a makeover. Invest in a great haircut and purge any colorful streaks (blue, pink, or purple anyone?). Girls, go to a great makeup counter and they will apply makeup (you don't have to buy everything).

And…though basic, I have to include:

- No visible tattoos
- Remove piercings with the exception of single ear piercings for women
- Make sure you have clean, styled hair—ditto for nails
- Women, wear makeup! Even if you like the natural look, you want to appear polished—mascara and lip gloss at a minimum
- Women, no minis
- Men, no white socks, short sleeved shirts, or polos
- No apparent designer labels—ditch the D&G, Chanel, Louis Vuittons in favor of a presentation folder or tote
- Women, no cleavage or exposed midriffs
- Women, no visible lingerie under sheer clothing
- No gum
- Believe it or not, everyone looks at shoes. They must be polished and stylish. Invest in a pair at Kenneth Cole, Nordstrom's, or Macy's. Women, no gladiator sandals, flats (unless you are wearing pants), or four-inch heels

• • •

**True Story:**
   Stan Richards, founder of The Richards Group, was interviewing a candidate for a creative position within his advertising agency. Stan said, "A young man in Dallas wanted very badly to work for us. He had gone to design school in Minneapolis and part of his final creative assignment was to design a costume—his was a tree. He actually wore that to the interview! It went downhill from there...."

. . .

## The Meeting
The easiest way to blow an interview is to be late. You should arrive ten to fifteen minutes early to give yourself enough time to get your game face on and make sure you've organized your materials (resume, references, bullet points, three-minute pitch, questions you want to ask, etc.). To arrive earlier makes the receptionist uneasy. To arrive late is unforgivable. Make sure you haven't eaten something that lingers (onion rings, garlic, etc.) and that your teeth are clean. Your hair should be combed and your clothes fresh and pressed. _You have 30 seconds to one minute to make a good first impression on your new boss._

The first few minutes are likely to be occupied with exchanging pleasantries. If you can find something in their office to comment on or ask about, it's a good icebreaker. This is a good time to start ascertaining the decision-making style of your prospective employer. Build rapport—you are simply meeting with someone. Above all, be yourself!

Next, the employer will likely take a look at your resume and ask you to tell him or her a little about yourself. This is

(a) a great opportunity to sell yourself in about three minutes (remember your three-minute pitch?) OR (b) a big, fat TRAP. This is where young candidates often talk and talk, and I find out much more than I asked. It is enlightening for me, but not necessarily the best start for them. Avoid your GPA or sorority/fraternity affiliation—*only share what you can relate to the job.*

At some point, you will be asked why you want the job, why you believe you are a good fit for the job, what led you to apply. This is the time to demonstrate what you've learned about the company and industry.

*Example:* "I know that you've just launched a new product and your competitive edge against Company ABC (their competition) is _____. I can bring a fresh perspective and am in the demographic your product is targeting."

OR

"Despite the economic challenges, I know your company is still a leader in the industry. I have a history of achieving goals regardless of outer circumstances as well...."

Your body language and actions will speak volumes. Men, keep both feet on the ground. Women can cross your legs if it doesn't take your skirt/dress up your legs to an inappropriate level. People who touch their hair or face, fiddle with something such as a pen, or who cannot maintain eye contact are all red flagged quickly.

## Questions You May Be Asked
I cannot give you every case scenario, but the following questions appear often when executives interview new candidates.

## What is your greatest strength?
Remember, tailor your answer to the job. For example, if the job involves sales, your answer should include customer needs analysis; if it involves customer service, you should include the fact that you work with different personalities well and like to resolve conflict, and so on.

And please, avoid "I'm a people person" at all costs—virtually everyone believes they are a "people person." It doesn't mean anything.

· · ·

## What is your greatest weakness?
No need for brutal self-assessment! Some safe answers might include, "Sometimes I am relentless in my desire to close a deal," or "At times I have a difficult time relaxing."

I have actually had a few candidates answer that they had difficulty with time management—they were being honest, but I mentally took them off my "A" list; I should not have to teach them basic time management.

· · ·

## What makes you the ideal candidate for this position?
"I always wanted to work here" or "I really need a job" are not good answers. Talk about how you can help the company—increase sales, lower costs, solve a problem.

· · ·

## What do you like about this job?
Give one or two strong examples; none should be location, security, insurance, or salary.

. . .

## How would you handle conflict on a team project?

. . .

## How do you stay on top of the latest research/trends?

. . .

## What's the most creative idea you've ever had?

. . .

## How do you learn from failure?  (Refer to "What's your greatest weakness?" as this is basically the same question, rephrased.)

. . .

## What are your goals and how do you plan to achieve them?

. . .

## Why did you choose your major?

. . .

## What are the two or three things most important to you in a position?

. . .

**What's been your greatest challenge?  How did you overcome it?**


**Give an example of a problem you solved and the process by which you solved it.**  Note:  A simple formula for this is (a) state the problem, (b) give relevant background information, (c) list your key traits/skills you used—remember the "What I'm Proudest of" and "What it Means," (d) recall the solution, and (e) relate what that solution achieved. This does not have to be business related.  At this point in your life, many of the problems you've solved are probably related to other situations.  Use an example you can tie back to what you can do for the company.

. . .


**What type of situations put you under pressure and how do you handle that pressure?**  You can think of your own situations. As to how you handle them, exercise is always a great answer.

. . .


**How would your friends describe you?  Your professors?**

. . .


**What challenges are you looking for in this position?**

. . .


**Are you willing to travel?  To relocate?**

. . .

**I have many candidates for this position.  Tell me why I should hire you over them.**

. . .

**What else should I know about you?**

. . .

> *True Story:*
>     Martin Birnbach, owner of Martin Birnbach & Assoc. executive search firm, offered this anecdote: "I interviewed a young graduate who said, 'I want to sell, but only in North Dallas so I don't have to drive much.'"

. . .

> *(Another) True Story:* (You can tell this is a hot topic for employers)
>     George Ellis, CFO, 360 Consulting, explained, "I had a young man interview whose resume and qualifications were great, but he wouldn't look me in they eye.  I introduced him to a few colleagues and they all thought he would be a great fit. So I hired him.  Within a few weeks, the whole department was out of whack—he just didn't fit in.  I learned to never ignore my instincts!"

. . .

**YOUR TURN:**

Now it's time for you to ask questions.  This is a step that you might overlook, but the employer will want to hear some questions that demonstrate your scope of knowledge of their industry as well as your maturity. After all, you aren't desperate to jump at any job opportunity; it needs to be a good fit for both the company and you.

You don't need more than five or six questions, so use them wisely. Here are some examples:

**How did you (employer) come to this field and position?**
People like to talk about themselves and this will help you when you are answering questions later.

• • •

**Who was the most successful person you've had in this position? What made them successful?**
Note: If you can get this question in early in the interview, you can use his or her answers to tailor your responses throughout your meeting.

• • •

**What are some of the immediate challenges facing your company/department?**
Then use your experiences to help him solve his or her problems.

• • •

**Where does this position fit within the company?**

• • •

**Is this a new position or, if not, who held it previously? Were they not successful or have they been promoted?**

. . .

**Does the company have any training for the position?**

. . .

**What process within the company is used for advancement?**

. . .

**Who will I be working with, reporting to?**

. . .

**NEVER** leave an interview without asking about next steps— **"When should I be hearing from you?"**

. . .

**"Do you need anything else from me before you make your decision?"**

. . .

**"What can I do to show you I'm the right person for this job?"**

. . .

**O**r make your own.  This is called CLOSING and you have to get comfortable with it.

At the end of any interview, IF and only IF the manager you've met has not indicated next steps for you within their organization (such as, "We do not currently have any openings, but will keep your resume on file"), ask the same questions: **"Do you know of anyone in the industry who is hiring?"**

If yes, **"Do you mind if I call them and use your name as an introduction?"**

## Last, Important Thoughts on the Interview

I believe that getting hired is a sales process. First, you have to establish rapport—or said more simply, make them like you. Next you have to establish their needs—you do this by asking questions, the most important of which is "Can you describe what you're looking for in the person you hire?" or "Can you describe your top performer in the department?" Third, use the answers to your questions to frame what you say to the interviewer, using some of his or her words in your answers (careful, not too many). In other words, he/she has told you what they need. You must make them believe you fill those needs via your skills, your experience, and/or your drive and attitude.

Last is the close. You ask for the job (if the interview has gone well and you truly believe you are a good match for the company and position)—"I like this company, its culture, its market position. And I've enjoyed meeting with you. I want the job…what do I have to do to be your top candidate?" It rarely works on the first go-round, but it sets you apart as someone focused and confident. Ask for next steps, "What's the next step in the process?" Then follow his or her directions. If you don't hear from them after one week, call the interviewer and ask to see them again. You should have a presentation in hand, a reason for this person to see you again.

## AND YOU THOUGHT <u>YOU</u> BLEW IT!

Let's have some fun!  As featured on a web site called PeterandTanya.com, here are some actual job interview quotes/ stories:

> Applicant refused to sit down and
> insisted on being interviewed standing up.

> • • •

> Candidate announced she hadn't had
> lunch and proceeded to eat a hamburger
> and fries in the interviewer's office.

> • • •

> Candidate said he never finished high
> school because he was kidnapped and
> kept in a closet in Mexico.

> • • •

> Balding candidate excused himself and
> returned a few minutes later wearing a
> hairpiece.

> • • •

> Applicant interrupted interview to phone
> her therapist for advice on how to answer
> specific interview questions.

> • • •

The employers were also asked to list the "most unusual" questions that have been asked by job candidates...

"What is it that you people do at this company?"

• • •

"What is the company motto?"

• • •

"Why aren't you in a more interesting business?"

• • •

"What are the zodiac signs of the board members?"

• • •

"Why do you want references?"

• • •

"Do I have to dress for the next interview?"

• • •

"Does your company have a policy regarding concealed weapons?"

• • •

Also included are a number of unusual statements made by candidates during the interview process...

"I feel uneasy indoors."

• • •

"Sometimes I feel like smashing things."

• • •

"I am fascinated by fire."

• • •

"I would have been more successful if nobody would have snitched on me."

• • •

"If the pay was right, I'd travel in a carnival."

• • •

# AFTER THE INTERVIEW

*"The greatest discovery of my generation is that human be-ings can alter their lives by altering their attitudes of mind."*

*William James*

• • •

Obviously, a thank you letter or hand-written note (my personal preference) is in order. Write notes in your Daily Log: what you learned from the person who interviewed you, your impressions, and so on. Then note a day in your calendar about a week after the interview to call and check in with the contact.

Better yet, send a proposal that highlights what you can do for the company, using what you learned in the interview as a starting point.

As you go through this process, there will be ups (you nailed the interview, they liked you, or you found the decision-maker and sent him an email) and lows (you have a day where you cannot seem to connect with anyone or the interview didn't go as well as you would have liked). So, two pieces of personal advice: take a break and do something fun—go shopping, play a round of basketball or golf, or go to a movie. This journey is not a straight line and you need times to regroup. Next, find your good attitude again. Desperation, impatience, and, at your worst, confrontation, never bode well with employers. They need good energy in their departments and it often goes further than skills!

If you're in the same city as your parents, now is a good time to do something for them. They have supported you for about twenty-two years and are your best advocates and cheerleaders. Especially if you are relying on them to support you until you land a job, offer to do something that will free up some time for them—yard work, cooking a good meal, grocery shopping, washing windows, etcetera. You get the idea.

It won't cost you money, and it will go a long way in showing them you are grateful for their support. (Sidebar: It will also give you something to do to keep your mind off the job hunt.)

# JOB ALTERNATIVES

*"When you come to the end of your rope, tie a knot and hang on."*

*Franklin D. Roosevelt*

• • •

**There's More Than One Road to Your Destination.**
When you started college, you no doubt had a dream job in mind. Hopefully, this book and the exercises you've done will help you do just that. In the event you cannot find placement in that job at this time, there are options:

- **Offer to do contract work or entry-level work to get your foot in the door.**

- **Teaching:** Starting salary: $40,000 (varies depending on school district and subject) Every city in America needs teachers. You can do a short training, begin teaching while you earn your certificate, and earn a paycheck while the industry you are prospecting recreates itself. Most school districts are desperate for math and science teachers as well as bilingual teachers.

- **Teach for America:** The same as above, but you agree to relocate anywhere in America. This is a great opportunity to help poor school districts in your own country—a great life experience as well. (www.teachforamerica.org)

- **Peace Corps:** This is one that's not for the faint of heart. You may end up in a village in Africa or Central America or Mexico. You can look at all of their locations at www.peacecorp.gov. Some notable alumni of this organization include Charlie Clifford, founder of Tumi Luggage; Patricia Cloherty, Chairperson US Russia Investment Fund; Samuel Gillespie III, Senior VP Exxon Mobile; Jan Guifarro, VP Corporate Communications, Colgate Palmolive; Frank Guzzetta, President, Ralph Lauren Home; Robert Haas, Chairperson of the Board, Levi Strauss; and Reed Hastings, founder and CEO of Netflix, to name a few.

- **Entrepreneurship:** America has a great history of entrepreneurs. And they seem to multiply when we are going through hard times! Here are some well-known companies that were started during a recession: Hyatt Corp (1957-58, Eisenhower recession), IHOP Corp (1958, Eisenhower recession), The Jim Henson Company (1958, Eisenhower recession), LexisNexis (1973, oil crisis/recession), CNN (1980, recession), General Electric (panic of 1873), and HP (at the end of the Great Depression).

There was a recent newspaper story of a man who'd lost his executive job in the mid-west. He had a family, mortgage, etc and had looked unsuccessfully for a job, any job, for months on end. He finally opened a shoe shine stand, which didn't make much money, but gave him a purpose and reinstated some much damaged pride. Then he opened another, and another. Now he's running his own successful business!

### Two College Entrepreneurial Stories:

Two college seniors, Terry Worrell and Dan Moran, worked together on a thesis that became a record store called Sound Warehouse in 1972. It grew into a national chain and was sold to Blockbuster in the 80's. It was their passion. They translated it into an extremely successful business.

Blake Mykoskie started EZ Laundry at SMU when he was just a sophomore. He believed the school needed an on-campus laundry service and hired sorority members to wear company branded t-shirts in exchange for dry cleaning. He quickly found his business growing to seven campuses and he was managing forty employees and eight trucks. Blake went on to found Tom's Shoes, a hugely successful shoe company that gives a pair of shoes to a child in a third world country for every pair purchased. Did he think this was what he would do when he was in college? Not likely!

Gailya Silhan

# LAST WORDS

*"Think of what you'd like your epitaph to  read – it's not likely to include your job!"*

*Gailya Silhan*

• • •

You and I are among the luckiest people on earth.  We are free, we won't go hungry, we don't have gunfire outside our windows or bombs blowing up in the streets.  We live in America.  And America is known globally as the place where, with hard work or a great idea, paupers can become millionaires.  It's true!

Having said that, I know you think finding your first job is the most important thing in the world.  But, in fact, the career you choose at this stage of your life may or may not be lasting.  Most people change jobs several times in their lifetime, and careers change at junctures like being laid off, a death in the family, or hitting a wall in their current job.  You will repeat the process of finding a job or changing companies many times, and the process will be very similar to what we've covered in this book.

I believe the most important decisions you will make have nothing to do with your job or career.  The friends you pick and love, the person you marry, and the ways in which you choose to give back to the world will determine your true happiness.  And, in the end, isn't that what we're all looking for?

Feel free to email me with questions or about your progress. You can reach me at gailya@collegejobcoach.com.

Happy trails.

# APPENDIX

*"The person who gets the farthest is generally the one who is willing to do and dare. The sure-thing boat never gets far from shore."*

*Dale Carnegie*

• • •

Gailya Silhan

## CHECKLIST

**EXERCISE ONE**

**EXERCISE TWO**

**EXERCISE THREE**

**EXERCISE FOUR**

**EXERCISE FIVE**

**EXERCISE SIX**

**THREE MINUTE PITCH**

**RESUME PROFESSIONALLY PRINTED**

**LIST OF COMPANIES YOU WILL RESEARCH**

**RESEARCH**

**BUSINESS CARDS PRINTED**

**PHONE CALLS – FIVE PER DAY MINIMUM**

**EMAILS TO DECISION MAKERS – FIVE PER DAY**

**THANK YOU NOTES – THE DAY OF INTERVIEW!**

**DAILY LOG COMPLETED EACH DAY**

78

**EXAMPLES:**

# RESUMÉ
# PETER D. MORRIS
1234 Knox St, Dallas, TX 75207
214.801.1234
pdmorris@gmail.com

---

My objective is to obtain a position as an auditor in a regional bank.

Experience:

2009-10     Treasurer, Economics Club, SMU
Responsible for ledger entry, monitoring fund raising activities, reporting and investment.  At end of term, our budget had grown from $10,000 to $13,250.

2007-09     Commercial Teller, Bank of America, Dallas TX
Worked with major business clients on deposits, statements, and resolution of account errors.

2006-07     Intern, Internal Revenue Service, Dallas
Input audit data, worked with agents to learn code and practiced review of tax returns.

2005        Teller, Oklahoma State Bank, OKC, OK
Worked directly with customers, including bilingual customers, at a regional bank. Reconciled my drawer daily.

Education:
SMU Cox School of Business
B.S. Finance, with minor in Economics

Other Interests:
Marathon running, Men With Ethics organization, Boys Club

Professional and Personal References Attached

Gailya Silhan

# THANK YOU LETTER

May 5, 2010


Ms. Diane Webster
Vice-President
Delta Bank
1234 Douglas St.
Dallas, TX 75218

Dear Ms. Webster,

Thank you so much for seeing me this afternoon. I appreciated both your time and your sharing of information about the job, the company culture, and exactly what you are looking for in a new employee.

My interest in the auditing job at Delta Bank increased after our interview. The nature of your client base (commercial) and the infrastructure you outlined are, I feel, a good match for my experience.

I hope to talk with you again soon. I have a passion for all things financial, am a hard worker, and will do everything within my power to earn your trust and respect.

Sincerely,


Peter D. Morris

Lists such as this one are published regularly, particularly online (i.e. www.money.cnn.com) or by Forbes:

1. **Walmart** – hiring to staff new locations.  Positions include information technology, research & development, human resources, marketing, finance and administration.

2. **Bank of America** – hiring small business & consumer banking positions as well as home loans, wealth management, technology, marketing & administrative.

3. **State Farm Insurance** – hiring new agents as well as accounting, legal, underwriting and claims.  Texas is one area of growth for the company.

4. **WellPoint** – accountants, actuaries, claims representatives, business analysts, marketing managers and account managers.

5. **UPS** – part time package handlers, sales representatives and IT professionals.

6. **Time Warner** – hiring marketing, media, finance, accounting, new media, film and television production and programming and more.

7. **Northrop Grumman** – hiring IT, engineering, production & manufacturing, product development, human resources and finance.

8. **Motorola** – hiring in sales, finance, project management and engineering.

9. **Abbott Laboratories** – hiring sales, IT, legal, engineering, clinical research and accounting.

10. **U.S. Government Jobs** – Safety Engineer (Dept of Labor), Budget Officer, Program Support Specialist, Safety and Occupational Health Specialist (Dept of Labor), Employee Benefits Law Specialist.  ALL government jobs can be found at www.usajobs.gov.

Gailya Silhan

# DAILY LOG

| DATE | COMPANY | POSITION | CONTACT NAME/ PHONE/EMAIL | NOTES |
|---|---|---|---|---|
| | | | | |
| | | | | |
| | | | | |
| | | | | |
| | | | | |
| | | | | |